M000013189

All Hail Hurricane Gordo

by

Carly Mensch

SAMUEL FRENCH

FOUNDED 1830

NEW YORK HOLLYWOOD LONDON TORONTO

SAMUELFRENCH.COM

Copyright © 2008 by Carly Mensch

ALL RIGHTS RESERVED

CAUTION: Professionals and amateurs are hereby warned that *ALL HAIL HURRICANE GORDO* is subject to a royalty. It is fully protected under the copyright laws of the United States of America, the British Commonwealth, including Canada, and all other countries of the Copyright Union. All rights, including professional, amateur, motion picture, recitation, lecturing, public reading, radio broadcasting, television and the rights of translation into foreign languages are strictly reserved. In its present form the play is dedicated to the reading public only.

The amateur live stage performance rights to *ALL HAIL HURRICANE GORDO* are controlled exclusively by Samuel French, Inc., and royalty arrangements and licenses must be secured well in advance of presentation. PLEASE NOTE that amateur royalty fees are set upon application in accordance with your producing circumstances. When applying for a royalty quotation and license please give us the number of performances intended, dates of production, your seating capacity and admission fee. Royalties are payable one week before the opening performance of the play to Samuel French, Inc., at 45 W. 25th Street, New York, NY 10010.

Royalty of the required amount must be paid whether the play is presented for charity or gain and whether or not admission is charged.

Stock royalty quoted upon application to Samuel French, Inc.

For all other rights than those stipulated above, apply to: The William Morris Agency, LLC, 1325 Avenue of the Americas, New York, NY 10019 Attn: Derek Zasky.

Particular emphasis is laid on the question of amateur or professional readings, permission and terms for which must be secured in writing from Samuel French, Inc.

Copying from this book in whole or in part is strictly forbidden by law, and the right of performance is not transferable.

Whenever the play is produced the following notice must appear on all programs, printing and advertising for the play: "Produced by special arrangement with Samuel French, Inc."

Due authorship credit must be given on all programs, printing and advertising for the play.

ISBN 978-0-573-66308-6   Printed in U.S.A.   #3179

No one shall commit or authorize any act or omission by which the copyright of, or the right to copyright, this play may be impaired.

No one shall make any changes in this play for the purpose of production.

Publication of this play does not imply availability for performance. Both amateurs and professionals considering a production are strongly advised in their own interests to apply to Samuel French, Inc., for written permission before starting rehearsals, advertising, or booking a theatre.

No part of this book may be reproduced, stored in a retrieval system, or transmitted in any form, by any means, now known or yet to be invented, including mechanical, electronic, photocopying, recording, videotaping, or otherwise, without the prior written permission of the publisher.

**IMPORTANT BILLING AND CREDIT
REQUIREMENTS**

All producers of *ALL HAIL HURRICANE GORDO* *must* give credit to the Author of the Play in all programs distributed in connection with performances of the Play, and in all instances in which the title of the Play appears for the purposes of advertising, publicizing or otherwise exploiting the Play and/or a production. The name of the Author *must* appear on a separate line on which no other name appears, immediately following the title and *must* appear in size of type not less than fifty percent of the size of the title type.

World premiere in the 2008 Humana Festival of New American Plays
Co-produced by Actors Theatre of Louisville and
The Cleveland Play House

actors theatre of louisville presents
32nd annual Humana Festival of New American Plays
made possible by a generous grant from The Humana Foundation

produced in association with The Cleveland Play House

All Hail Hurricane Gordo

by **Carly Mensch**
directed by **Sean Daniels**

March **13 – 30, 2008**

THE CAST

Chaz	**Matthew Dellapina***
Gordo	**Patrick James Lynch***
India	**Tracee Chimo***
Oscar	**William McNulty***

The suburbs of New York.

There will be one 15-minute intermission.

Presented by special arrangement with William Morris Agency, LLC

Scenic Designer	**Paul Owen**
Costume Designer	**Lorraine Venberg**
Lighting Designer	**Deb Sullivan**
Sound Designer	**Matt Callahan**
Properties Designer	**Mark Walston**
Fight Supervisor	**Lee Look**
Stage Manager	**Paul Mills Holmes***
Assistant Stage Manager	**Captain Kate Murphy***
Dramaturg	**Julie Felise Dubiner**
Casting	**Emily Ruddock**

Director underwritten by Fran and Don Berg

*Member of Actors' Equity Association, the union of professional actors and stage managers of the United States.

actorstheatre

THE CLEVELAND PLAY HOUSE

PRESENTS
IN ASSOCIATION WITH
ACTORS THEATRE OF LOUISVILLE

MICHAEL BLOOM ARTISTIC DIRECTOR
KEVIN MOORE MANAGING DIRECTOR

ALL HAIL HURRICANE GORDO

BY CARLY MENSCH

SCENIC DESIGNER
PAUL OWEN

COSTUME DESIGNER
LORRAINE VENBERG

LIGHTING DESIGNER
DEB SULLIVAN

SOUND DESIGNER
MATT CALLAHAN

FIGHT SUPERVISOR
LEE COOK

STAGE MANAGER
AMANDA HARLAND

CASTING
EMILY RUDDOCK

DIRECTED BY SEAN DANIELS

APRIL 18 - MAY 11, 2008
DRURY THEATRE

IN PROMOTIONAL PARTNERSHIP WITH
THE PLAIN DEALER

The Cleveland Play House's Production Staff is responsible for the sets, costumes, lighting, props, furniture, scenic painting, sound, special effects, and/or wigs used in this production.

Ohio Arts Council
A STATE AGENCY
THAT SUPPORTS PUBLIC
PROGRAMS IN THE ARTS

CUYAHOGA ARTS
AND CULTURE

CHARACTERS

CHAZ, late 20s
GORDO, mid 20s
INDIA, 18
OSCAR, late 50s

SETTING

A ranch-style house in a waning suburb of New York. The living
room has been converted into a makeshift office.

For my brother

1.

(A living room turned makeshift office. Two desks, one neat and organized with a typewriter and carefully arranged stacks of paper and the other a total wreck, purgatory-like, where things half-eaten and half-assed take up residence – opened bags of chips, abandoned Tinker Toy projects, wrinkled Wrestlemania magazines, parts of an old Bingo set, a bug collection in a recycled yogurt container, swimming goggles, etc. There is a worn-out couch dead center covered with piles and piles of phone books and a lone wooden chair in the corner.)

(CHAZ, late 20s, sits at the neat desk. Shirt and tie. Typing. Enter GORDO, mid 20s. In boxers and a little boys pajama top. CHAZ continues typing. GORDO watches for a moment.)

GORDO. Hey.

(Type type. Type type.)

Hey Chaz.

(CHAZ doesn't respond. GORDO patiently repeats himself.)

Chaz. Chaz. Chaz.

CHAZ. I hear you.

GORDO. You want breakfast?

CHAZ. Already ate.

GORDO. Alright.

(GORDO exits. CHAZ pulls out the sheet of paper from the typewriter and puts it into an envelope. He finds the appropriate address in one of the phone books open on his desk.)

(GORDO returns with some old mush in Tupperware. He loiters around CHAZ's desk while he eats.)

GORDO. Mmm.

CHAZ. What is that?

GORDO. Stir-fry.

CHAZ. From last week?

GORDO. I guess.

CHAZ. You didn't see any cereal?

*(**GORDO** shrugs.)*

I bought some yesterday.

GORDO. You bought the bad kind.

CHAZ. I bought Cheerios.

GORDO. You bought Shit-e-os. The kind in the plastic bag. The kind you have to crawl on the floor of the supermarket to get. They look like Cheerios but surprise – they're really Shit-e-os. Simple mistake. How long you been working?

CHAZ. Little over an hour.

GORDO. Jeez. That's discipline.

CHAZ. Just finished the fourth one this morning. Oh. And we need to pick up more stamps. We're running low.

GORDO. Look at you. You're like this self-guided missile. Like your brain is on autopilot.

CHAZ. It's after ten by the way.

GORDO. See? You've even got an internal clock.

CHAZ. We start at nine thirty.

GORDO. *We?*

CHAZ. The household.

GORDO. Yeah…I can't get up then. Sorry.

CHAZ. Why not?

GORDO. Because. You got rid of the TV. That's how I used to tell time – the channel guide. I used to watch the channel guide every morning until breakfast. Do you know you can basically schedule your entire life just by watching the channel guide? It tells you what's on and when and how long, and there's even a little ticking clock in the upper hand corner. But now it's just…nothing. I'm a little ship, lost at sea, all floating around. Where's my compass? Where's my best friend? Oh yeah, Chaz sold it on eBay.

CHAZ. I didn't sell it on eBay. I sold it to Kip Bearman.

GORDO. The guy from the Y?

CHAZ. Yeah.

GORDO. Now what's he gonna do with a TV? Smoke it?

CHAZ. *(amused)* Please tell me how you smoke a television set.

GORDO. Oh he'll figure out a way. He'll probably pull out all the wires and try to snort the electricity out of them.

CHAZ. What makes you think he does drugs? We see him at the pool, that's it.

GORDO. And on the bench outside, waiting for the bus. Smoking Lucky Strikes. Every Wednesday, just sitting on the bench. Smoking.

CHAZ. Cigarettes.

GORDO. Cigarettes are a drug, man. They've got nicotine. You smoke one and Bang! your brain is a plate of scrambled eggs. Haven't you seen the commercials? Don't ever smoke, Chaz. Promise me you'll never smoke.

CHAZ. It's a little late for me to take up smoking, don't you think?

GORDO. *Promise* me, Chaz.

CHAZ. Fine. I promise.

GORDO. Promise.

CHAZ. I said I promise.

GORDO. You can't die on me.

CHAZ. I'm not dying.

GORDO. I'm just saying, you better not.

(a moment)

I'm thinking of writing a letter. To Child Protective Services. With a note that says, "Dear Protective Services.

Question: Do you really protect every child in America? Answer: No. You don't. Love, Gordon. P.S. Can you please get me a new TV?"

*(**CHAZ** just stares at him.)*

CHAZ. Why don't you go get dressed. Your leg hair – it's blinding me.

GORDO. You don't think that's funny? Writing a letter to Child Protective Services?

CHAZ. It's not that funny anymore.

GORDO. You write letters.

CHAZ. That's different.

GORDO. You write like ten a day.

CHAZ. I write inquiries. It's a different thing.

GORDO. I can sign both our names. They might like that – a two for one deal.

(noticing)

GORDO. What's up with the tie?

CHAZ. Oh. Right.

GORDO. You look good. You look like you're going to court.

CHAZ. I've…got a meeting today. We both do, actually.

GORDO. Ah…we're auctioning off the couch. First the TV, now the couch. Everything must go!

CHAZ. We're not selling anything. It's – an interview.

GORDO. What kind of interview?

CHAZ. You know, an interview.

GORDO. Okay. But what kind?

CHAZ. You can't get upset.

GORDO. What? Are you getting another job?

CHAZ. Not me. Someone else. Coming here.

GORDO. Someone who?

CHAZ. Someone who's coming here to interview with us.

GORDO. Why would they do that?

CHAZ. Go get dressed and we'll talk all about it. And put on a nice shirt – you can borrow one of mine if you want. With a collar.

GORDO. No. Tell me now, Chaz.

CHAZ. It's no big deal. It's just a meeting.

GORDO. Tell me what's going on.

CHAZ. Not if you're going to freak out.

GORDO. I'M NOT GOING TO FREAK OUT. Just tell me already.

*(**CHAZ** composes himself.)*

CHAZ. A potential tenant. She's coming in at eleven.

GORDO. Today?

CHAZ. Yeah.

*(**GORDO** processes all this.)*

GORDO. Okay.

CHAZ. Yeah?

GORDO. Uh huh.

*(Beat. **GORDO** exits to his room. **CHAZ** watches the door warily. A few seconds later, **GORDO** re-enters wearing a football helmet. **CHAZ** stares at him for a moment.)*

CHAZ. Gordon.

*(**GORDO** stares back.)*

Gordo.

*(**GORDO** lowers his head like a bull.)*

Don't do this.

*(**GORDO** kicks invisible dirt as if preparing to charge.)*

I said don't.

*(**GORDO** charges. Rams **CHAZ** in the stomach. **CHAZ** falls down.)*

OFF! Off. Get OFF!

GORDO. AAGGHHH!!!!

CHAZ. Jesus.

(**CHAZ** *tries to wiggle out from beneath* **GORDO**.)

CHAZ. I said off.

GORDO. I'M GOING TO BREAK YOUR ARM.

CHAZ. I need my arm.

GORDO. NO YOU DON'T.

CHAZ. Please. I do.

GORDO. NO. NO MORE ARM.

CHAZ. You know what time it is? I think you know what time it is.

GORDO. TIME TO DIE?

CHAZ. What?

GORDO. TIME TO EAT MY FACE!

(**CHAZ** *manages to break free. Stands up.*)

CHAZ. I think it's time for a time out.

GORDO. No.

CHAZ. Yes. Time out. Go sit in the chair.

GORDO. I don't want to sit in the chair.

CHAZ. You just head butt me in the goddamn stomach. I've probably got internal bleeding. Go have time out.

GORDO. Fine.

(**GORDO** *goes to the lone wooden chair and takes a seat.*)

GORDO. How long?

CHAZ. Two minutes.

GORDO. One.

CHAZ. Fine.

(**GORDO** *sits in the chair. Counts quietly to himself.* **CHAZ** *brings* **GORDO**'*s empty container into the kitchen.*)

CHAZ. *(as he goes)* I think you actually ruptured my spleen this time.

(When he returns, **CHAZ** *looks at his watch.)*

58...59...60.

(GORDO stands up.)

Are you ready to talk about this like a grown-up?

GORDO. Uh huh.

CHAZ. Are you sure?

GORDO. I'm calm now. See?

CHAZ. Why don't you take off the helmet?

GORDO. It's the San Diego Chargers.

CHAZ. I know.

GORDO. Okay.

    (**GORDO** *takes off the helmet.*)

I don't know why I get so angry.

CHAZ. You've got stuff you're dealing with.

GORDO. But we've both got the same stuff.

CHAZ. I think you've also got some kind of anger management problem, maybe.

GORDO. Like elephants?

CHAZ. Yeah. Like elephants.

GORDO. Goring people in Asia, trampling entire villages in Africa. It's a worldwide epidemic you know. The whole animal kingdom's striking out.

    (*beat*)

You're not angry?

CHAZ. Not really.

GORDO. I don't want to be so angry all the time.

CHAZ. I know.

GORDO. It just comes out.

CHAZ. Well you've got to work on that. People aren't going to just accept that kind of behavior out in the real world. That's what got you into trouble, remember?

GORDO. Yeah.

CHAZ. You can't just do whatever you feel like. You're a human being. There are certain boundaries.

GORDO. You told me to always be myself.

CHAZ. Well. Not when your self is fiery ball of rage – okay? That's when you make an exception.

    (*beat*)

GORDO. Can we talk about this person now?

CHAZ. Sure.

GORDO. You're sick of talking to me, is that it?

CHAZ. Yeah. I'm sick of talking to you. That's it.

GORDO. You think I'm boring?

CHAZ. That's not even a possibility.

GORDO. You want me to fade into the darkness like some kind of phantasm.

CHAZ. I want you to be just a little more understanding, that's what I want.

GORDO. I'm very understanding. Trust me, I understand stuff.

CHAZ. I mean more understanding of me. Of what I need. I have needs too you know. I'm not just your babysitter.

(**GORDO** *chuckles.*)

I'm glad you find that so entertaining. Besides – It's not just that. It's also – money stuff.

GORDO. Why? What happened?

CHAZ. Nothing happened.

GORDO. Are we in the red, Chaz?

CHAZ. We could use the extra income, that's all.

GORDO. You're supposed to tell me when we're in the red, Chaz.

CHAZ. We're not in the red.

GORDO. What about all the money I made at the airport?

CHAZ. You worked there for maybe three weeks.

GORDO. And not just that. I've had a lot of jobs, man.

CHAZ. Oh I know.

GORDO. The library –

CHAZ. Two libraries – you've worked at two of them.

GORDO. Sal's.

CHAZ. I forgot about Sal's.

GORDO. They gave me free meatball subs at Sal's.

CHAZ. Yeah, and it made you fat.

GORDO. What about when I gave people tours of the neighborhood and pretended that Amelia Earhart grew up here? I taught them all how to make paper airplanes so they'd have souvenirs to take back with them.

CHAZ. That doesn't count because you didn't charge them anything. In fact, you actually spent money because of all the paper.

GORDO. That was pretty funny though, right?

CHAZ. It was a little funny.

GORDO. What about you?

CHAZ. Oh – cause two jobs isn't bad enough.

GORDO. Do three.

CHAZ. Don't you think I'm pulling enough weight here already?

GORDO. You wake up at the crack of dawn. You're up anyway.

CHAZ. I get up early to do my personal business.

GORDO. So I'll do that stuff. What – it's just writing letters and stuffing them into envelopes, right? I can do that.

CHAZ. You can't. It's my personal – it's something I do for myself, okay? It's mine. Besides – we wouldn't be in this situation if someone hadn't gotten himself fired from maybe the easiest job on the entire planet and probably blacklisted from the entire global job market.

GORDO. Hey –

CHAZ. It's true. I don't think anyone's going to hire you now. They've probably tagged you in the system.

GORDO. What system?

CHAZ. The internet…job system.

(beat)

GORDO. So this person. It's a girl?

CHAZ. Her name is India.

GORDO. What? Like the country?

CHAZ. Yeah.

GORDO. That's messed up.

CHAZ. She sounds nice.

GORDO. She's probably a gypsy.

CHAZ. Probably not.

GORDO. So what. Are you going to marry her?

CHAZ. I've never even met her.

GORDO. You said she was nice.

CHAZ. I talked to her on the phone.

GORDO. You can't marry her.

CHAZ. Who said I was? She'd be our *tenant.*

GORDO. Can't.

CHAZ. And who are you to tell me who I can and cannot marry?

GORDO. Can't. Can't do it.

CHAZ. Yeah, you've said that. But why not?

GORDO. Because.

CHAZ. Because…?

GORDO. Because. *(beat)* I'm disabled.

CHAZ. You are NOT disabled.

GORDO. I am. I have a social disorder.

CHAZ. You do not. It's all in your head.

GORDO. I have Asperger's. I looked it up.

CHAZ. How many fingers am I holding up right now?

(He holds up two fingers.)

GORDO. Four?

CHAZ. You do not have Asperger's.

GORDO. You can't just go off with some girl and leave me alone.

CHAZ. I'm not going anywhere.

GORDO. Promise?

CHAZ. How can I go anywhere? I've got to fucking watch you like a hawk.

GORDO. You don't have to watch me.

CHAZ. Are you kidding? What if you pull another stunt like you just did? What if you grab onto some stranger's

ankles at the supermarket? What if you run away and
hide out in a tool shed for the next five years eating
nothing but paint chips and throwing pebbles at baby
animals? Watch you? You might as well be made of
cement and glued to the bottom of all my shoes the
way things are.

(Pause. Feels bad.)

Now how bout you go change.

GORDO. I should shower first. If I'm going to put on clean
clothes.

CHAZ. Great idea. Why don't you go take a shower.

GORDO. I'm not going to use any soap. You got the liquid
kind. There's no lather.

CHAZ. That's fine. Even if you just rinse yourself. That's
fine.

GORDO. Okay.

(GORDO starts to exit.)

GORDO. Hey Chaz.

CHAZ. Yeah?

GORDO. You're a good brother. You take good care of me.

(pause)

CHAZ. Don't forget the pants. Maybe your corduroys. Something nice.

GORDO. Yeah. Okay.

(GORDO starts to exit. CHAZ holds up the envelope.)

CHAZ. Wait. Mail.

*(GORDO goes over to his desk and picks up a plastic bin
from the floor that says US MAIL. He carries it over to
CHAZ who places the envelope inside.)*

GORDO. I'm on it, bro.

(GORDO exits with the bin. Blackout.)

2.

(CHAZ sits at his desk. Across from him is INDIA, a self-styled rebel with a blue streak in her hair, in GORDO's time out chair. There is a backpack and an instrument case – a French horn case – on the floor at her feet.)

CHAZ. Can I get you something to drink?

INDIA. Is it appropriate to make drink requests during an interview?

CHAZ. If you're thirsty.

INDIA. I'm not really, but if you have Orangina, I guess I would have that.

CHAZ. I don't think we have any Orangina.

INDIA. Then no. I'm not thirsty.

CHAZ. Alright. How about hobbies?

INDIA. Hobbies?

CHAZ. Yeah.

INDIA. Tough question.

CHAZ. I mean, aside from music obviously.

INDIA. What, because all young people like music?

CHAZ. I just meant, your instrument. *(gestures to her instrument case)*

INDIA. Oh. The horn. Right. I play the horn. Duh. Not all the time though, don't worry. I won't just randomly break out playing the horn.

(a slight pause)

CHAZ. How about movies? That might be easier.

INDIA. Favorite movies?

CHAZ. Sure.

INDIA. Like top ten or just a few?

CHAZ. Just name anything.

INDIA. I like this movie called The Devils, how's that?

CHAZ. I've never heard of it.

INDIA. It stars Vanessa Redgrave as a sex-crazed hunchback nun. I guess you'd call it a gothic porno. But there's also this whole historical backdrop too. It's pretty insane.

CHAZ. I'll have to ask my brother – he's really into movies.

INDIA. *(looking around)* I thought this place would be dirtier for some reason. Or even just a little seedy.

CHAZ. The house?

INDIA. From the ad. I had this picture in my head – with broken beer bottles everywhere and dial-up that takes thirty minutes just to get on to the internet. Because it's *so* cheap.

CHAZ. Is it?

INDIA. Five hundred bucks? That would probably get you like a broom closet in Manhattan.

CHAZ. Should I have asked for more?

INDIA. Are you kidding? That's your whole selling point. Besides, I'm like *so* poor right now.

(beat)

INDIA. Is this even normal? Being interviewed to rent a room?

CHAZ. I've never rented a room before.

INDIA. It's just that, these questions are getting kind of personal. You're not interviewing me as a person, right? You're interviewing me as a kind of a potential…financial arrangement.

CHAZ. Woah.

INDIA. I'm just saying.

CHAZ. You want to get a sense of what a person's like – if you're going to live with them.

INDIA. Isn't that weird? That we might live together.

CHAZ. Not together. Next to one another. Across the hall actually.

INDIA. *(smiling)* Right.

(a small pause)

INDIA. What about you? Do I get to ask you any questions?

CHAZ. *(trying to make a joke)* Who's conducting the interview, am I right?

(INDIA *doesn't laugh. Just stares at him.)*

I'm kidding. Of course.

INDIA. Okay. Let me think. Okay. How about…Are you from here originally?

CHAZ. Yes.

INDIA. Do you always wear a tie?

CHAZ. No.

INDIA. What about…how do you feel about the service sector in general?

CHAZ. The service sector?

INDIA. Of the economy.

CHAZ. It's – I guess it's a major part of our economy? Why – how do you feel about it?

INDIA. I hate it.

CHAZ. The whole thing?

INDIA. People groveling on the ground, scrubbing other people's shoes and whatnot. It's just seems so demeaning.

CHAZ. That's a very…interesting point of view.

INDIA. No, it's not. You don't have to lie.

CHAZ. I'm not. I'm sorry – I don't know what else to say.

INDIA. You don't have to say anything. You can just roll your eyes if you want. When I talk. I won't be offended.

CHAZ. Why would I roll my eyes?

INDIA. I don't know. But if you want to.

(beat)

INDIA. Look. Can I level with you, Mr –

CHAZ. Chaz.

INDIA. This place, Chaz. It's pretty much exactly what I'm looking for.

CHAZ. Well that's great –

INDIA. But the whole set-up – let's just both admit – a little on the creepy side. Two guys working at home. Alone. Asking for someone to come live with them in their weirdo home office slash bachelor pad in bumblefuck, New York. But I'm fine with that. In fact, I kind of like it. The ambiguity. The sense that anything could happen. It's so…exciting. Like there could be dead bodies hidden in the walls, like in that Edgar Alan Poe story with the heart, the one that keeps beating even after the guy is dead, keeps haunting him, haunting his thoughts, his ability to function. And that's totally fine with me. I'm willing to take that risk. But maybe not everyone is, right? Maybe not everyone is as openly adventurous and liberal-minded as I am.

(pause)

How'd I do? Did I get it?

*(**CHAZ** just stares at her for a moment.)*

CHAZ. How…old…are you?

(a slight pause)

INDIA. Twenty-four. But I didn't go to college.

*(Enter **GORDO**. Showered, but still wearing his boxers and pajama top, except with a tie and dress shoes.)*

INDIA. Hi. I'm India.

GORDO. You're in my chair.

CHAZ. Come on. We're in the middle of something.

GORDO. She can do it somewhere else. That's my chair.

CHAZ. We don't have any other chairs.

GORDO. She can sit on the couch. It's a perfectly sit-table piece of furniture.

CHAZ. *(to **INDIA**)* I'm sorry.

INDIA. It's fine. I didn't mean to take his seat.

CHAZ. You didn't –

(She gets up.)

GORDO. *(taking the chair)* Thanks.

(He returns the chair to its usual corner. Doesn't sit it in.

Just leaves it there.)

INDIA. So you're the other brother?

GORDO. I'm Gordo.

INDIA. And you're his brother?

GORDO. I'm not some kind of side-show. I'm the idea man. I come up with the ideas.

INDIA. The ideas for what?

GORDO. I'm like an electric guitar. Thoughts shoot out of my head like amps and bounce off the walls and hit random people in the audience. And they're like *Help, oh my God, that guy's brilliant idea just zapped me!* And I'm like *Sorry babe, I can't help it for being so electrifyingly brilliant.*

CHAZ. He doesn't actually play the guitar.

GORDO. I used to work at Blockbuster, stocking shelves. I even had my own shelf, "Gordon recommends," which I changed every week so people could follow along. But Chaz thought it was a waste of my talent. That's why I don't work there any more. Oh, and I did something kind of bad. Well, not really bad…But. So now Chaz kind of takes care of me. We're this amazing us-against-the-world dynamic duo. We defy all of Western Civilization's accepted patterns of behavior.

CHAZ. *(To GORDO)* Why don't you go change so you can join us for the rest of the interview?

GORDO. I already changed.

CHAZ. No. You added a tie.

GORDO. And shoes.

CHAZ. I told you to borrow one of my shirts.

GORDO. None of them went with the tie.

INDIA. I don't care if he wears pajamas.

GORDO. See?

CHAZ. You shouldn't encourage him.

INDIA. I'm just saying – I don't believe in dress codes in general.

CHAZ. It's not a code – it's about getting in the habit of being semi-presentable.

GORDO. I don't believe in dress codes, either.

CHAZ. What a surprise. Here, India, why don't we move our conversation over to the couch.

INDIA. Okay.

(CHAZ and INDIA make their way over to the couch.)

GORDO. Watch out. There's anthrax.

INDIA. Where?

GORDO. In the couch.

CHAZ. He's lying.

GORDO. Bacteria overload – we haven't cleaned it in years.

CHAZ. Just ignore him – really, he's harmless.

GORDO. I'm an elephant. I trample entire villages.

CHAZ. Well then. I guess I stand corrected.

GORDO. I kill civilians with my massive tusks.

CHAZ. That's right. You're an animal, Gordo. You're a big fat hairy animal. I'm so glad that you've chosen to tell India about that. You should be really proud of yourself. Really. Bravo.

GORDO. *(a little hurt)* Yeah, whatever.

(GORDO takes a seat at his desk. He grinds the ball cage slowly while the others talk.)

(CHAZ clears off some phone books from the couch.)

INDIA. Lot of phone books.

CHAZ. Something I'm working on. You can just throw them on the floor.

(She does. They take a seat on the couch.)

CHAZ. So…you were saying you didn't go to college?

INDIA. Nope.

CHAZ. Neither did I. Or rather, I didn't graduate.

INDIA. College is for suckers. It's just a big coming out party for rich kids and conformists.

CHAZ. I made it through most of my first year, but there were extenuating circumstances.

(**GORDO** *grinds the cage really loudly.*)

(*He stops.*)

GORDO. How come she has bags with her?

(**GORDO** *gets up and goes over to* **INDIA**.)

GORDO. Why did you bring bags to an interview?

INDIA. I thought…you had a spare room.

GORDO. Yeah…but did Chaz already tell you can have it? He did. Didn't he. Of course he did.

CHAZ. I didn't say anything.

GORDO. Chazenstein, that's what I'm gonna start calling you – Dr. Chazenstein. Cooking up all these schemes like some sort of Mad Scientist.

CHAZ. Fine. Call me whatever.

GORDO. I will.

CHAZ. Good.

GORDO. Yeah, we'll see about that.

(**GORDO** *exits to his room.*)

(**CHAZ** *and* **INDIA** *sit in silence for a moment.*)

INDIA. So you *do* have a spare room, right?

CHAZ. We do. I'm sorry. He's not always like this.

INDIA. I don't mind if it smells like old person or whatever.

CHAZ. It's been empty for about twelve years now.

INDIA. Oh. Okay. Wow.

(**CHAZ** *stands up and goes over to his desk.*)

CHAZ. I don't really have a contract for you. But I typed up a list of terms…

INDIA. So I got it!?

CHAZ. If you're still comfortable. Given what you've witnessed.

INDIA. Don't worry. I can totally take care of myself. I'm a yellow belt in tae kwon doe and I once cursed off this homeless guy who had been following me for like ten blocks.

CHAZ. And you said you can pay by cash, right?

INDIA. I've got it with me now. In my backpack. I can give it to you right now if you want.

(A moment while he decides.)

CHAZ. Okay.

*(**INDIA** pulls out a wad of cash from her backpack.)*

INDIA. Here's the first month. I'll have more later, obviously.

*(**CHAZ** takes the money.)*

CHAZ. Great.

*(She extends her hand. **CHAZ** shakes it.)*

INDIA. That was easy.

(beat)

INDIA. I'm going to go brush my teeth now.

CHAZ. Okay…

INDIA. I'm not compulsive or anything. I just didn't brush them this morning.

CHAZ. Sure. I understand.

INDIA. I don't know where the bathroom is.

CHAZ. The lock's broken. There's a book propping it shut.

INDIA. Thanks.

(She picks up the instrument case and heads towards the bathroom.)

INDIA. And thanks for taking a chance on me. I'll be really good. I promise.

CHAZ. I'm excited to have you here. Both of us. We've never had a roommate before. I mean we've thought about it. I've thought about it. It's been a long time since we've had company of any sort. But. So yeah. It's really exciting. I'm, we're, very excited.

*(**INDIA** smiles. Exits. **CHAZ** walks around. Excited.)*

(Beat.)

(A loud crashing noise, like a bull running into a wall.)

(Lights fade.)

3.

(The next day.)

*(**GORDO** sits at his desk, playing Bingo by himself. This is a difficult maneuver, however, because one of his arms is now in a sling. Something crudely improvised. A bed sheet maybe. Or a tablecloth.)*

*(Enter **INDIA**. She stands in the doorway and watches him. **GORDO** seems not to notice. He spins the metal cage. Spin spin. Spin spin.)*

GORDO. B5.

(Puts a plastic marker on one of his cards. Spins the cage.)

N36

(Puts plastic markers on two of his cards. Spins.)

G52

(Consults his cards. Doesn't have it.)

Hmmm. What about…G…53? Oh. Will you look at that?

(Puts a marker on G53 without looking up)

I see you standing there.

INDIA. Oh. I – Is Chaz here?

GORDO. He's gone.

INDIA. Gone?

GORDO. Out.

INDIA. Out where?

GORDO. He's stocking up on nuts for winter. Want in?

INDIA. On Bingo?

GORDO. Here. I'll give you a head start.

*(**GORDO** passes her one of the cards he's been playing with. They play.)*

GORDO. G47

(*Neither one has it.* **GORDO** *spins again.*)

O75

INDIA. Can you please pass me a chip?

GORDO. You don't have it.

INDIA. Uh. Yes I do.

GORDO. No. I said G 75.

INDIA. You said O.

GORDO. No. I said G. As in Guantanamo. Or Gypsy.

(**GORDO** *puts a marker on his board*)

Which gives me…Oh look. Bingo.

(**GORDO** *clears off his board so that she can't contest it.*)

GORDO. It's not your fault. I'm really good at this.

INDIA. I thought Bingo was one of those luck games.

GORDO. Lies. I beat Chaz every time.

INDIA. Oh. Does he usually play with you?

GORDO. Sometimes. Not lately. But.

You know.

INDIA. I'm an only child.

GORDO. Okay.

INDIA. I used to pretend I had an older brother. You know how kids create imaginary friends for themselves? I named him Macintosh because we had just gotten this computer – an Apple IIGS – and I spent *hours* playing this game called Number Munchers where this little green monster eats away at really basic math problems. My parents were really worried for a while – they thought naming a make-believe person after a computer operating systems wasn't "imaginative" enough. But then I was really good at painting so that made them happy.

GORDO. Me and Chaz. This one time – We painted a dog.

INDIA. You what?

GORDO. We took this dog and we painted it.

INDIA. Oh my god.

GORDO. We found all this yellow paint in the garage so we just covered it all over our neighbor's Rottweiler, Einstein. He looked like a giant egg McMuffin.

INDIA. That's pretty intense.

GORDO. We used to get into a lot of mischief. Like for example, this other time, we stapled bologna to all the trees in the neighborhood. Oscar Meyer All-American Beef. Because we were so sick of having to eat the same crappy bologna and Kraft sandwiches every day for lunch. See, our mom didn't know how to cook. Or didn't believe in it. It wasn't like a feminist thing. It was like a nurturing thing. She was anti-nurturing in general.

INDIA. Well… At least you had Chaz as some sort of partner in crime. Not everyone has that sort of thing.

GORDO. Yeah. But then one day he just stopped doing all that stuff. Like it was cut out of him. Now he's so serious all the time. Daddy Chaz. I don't know if you've noticed.

INDIA. He's a little uptight. I was secretly hoping to show up here and find some guy all covered in tattoos and maybe even like moderately illiterate, instead of just some nice normal person wearing a tie. But Chaz seems cool. In his own semi-nerdy way.

GORDO. He's the best. He basically raised me by himself.

INDIA. What about your parents?

GORDO. You mean "Those of which we never speak?" They might be dead. We don't know. It's one of those "where-are-they-now?" situations. Like on VH1.

(beat)

INDIA. What happened to your arm?

GORDO. I hurt it.

INDIA. How?

GORDO. Wrestling my demons. They were hiding under the bed so I just, grr, you know.

*(**INDIA** looks at him – really?)*

I ran into a wall. Busted my shoulder.

INDIA. For fun?

GORDO. It's just something I do.

INDIA. You just run into things?

GORDO. I have trouble controlling my emotions sometimes. That's why I keep getting fired.

INDIA. Do you have…

GORDO. A helmet?

INDIA. No. I mean…have you seen anyone about this?

GORDO. No thank you. Me and Chaz, we don't need anyone else. We operate outside the social order. Plus, we figure they might take me away. If we tell somebody.

INDIA. Who would take you away?

GORDO. …The authorities.

(beat)

GORDO. I don't know where Chaz is.

INDIA. Do you usually keep tabs on his whereabouts?

GORDO. You said you were looking for him.

INDIA. Not *looking* for him.

GORDO. Everyone thinks it's The Chaz Show – All Chaz, All the Time. But I'm the brains of the operation. I'm the guy hiding behind the velvet curtain. *(beat)* Boo!

*(**INDIA** jumps.)*

That was me, coming out from behind the curtain.

INDIA. You got me.

GORDO. We're like one of those famous teams. Butch Cassidy and the Sundance Kid. Mick Jagger and Keith Richards. Beethoven and Beethoven's brother.

INDIA. I didn't know Beethoven had a brother.

GORDO. See? He had two. Caspar and Nikolaus. I forgot Caspar's story, but Nikolaus was an apothecary who collected people's brains in glass jars.

(beat)

Do I scare you?

INDIA. Not really.

GORDO. Are you sure?

INDIA. Why do you want me to be afraid of you?

GORDO. I don't wear deodorant. Sometimes I wear the same clothes for weeks. Months maybe.

(**INDIA** *stares at him.*)

INDIA. You're pretty weird, you know that? Both of you. The way you talk about yourself and then Chaz, being this mysterious writer guy.

GORDO. Chaz isn't a writer.

INDIA. He's not?

GORDO. No. He just writes letters. He goes through these phone books and writes letters to people. Hundreds and hundreds of letters.

INDIA. And who are the people he writes letters to?

(**GORDO** *doesn't respond.*)

INDIA. So what – Do you just sit around this house all day?

GORDO. I'm pretty busy

INDIA. Do you do any chores?

GORDO. Not really.

INDIA. Not at all?

GORDO. We abolished them a long time ago.

INDIA. So who cleans your house?

GORDO. It self-cleans. It's a self-cleaning house.

(**INDIA** *lifts a pair of goggles off of* **GORDO**'s *desk.*)

GORDO. Goggles. For swimming.

INDIA. Where do you swim?

GORDO. At the Y. Mondays Wednesdays and Fridays. I get to use the pool for free because Chaz works there. He teaches random stuff. But mostly tennis. To disabled kids. What about you? Do you swim?

INDIA. He teaches tennis?

GORDO. To disabled kids.

INDIA. That's really sweet.

GORDO. Nah. It'd just cause he's not so good anymore.
And, it's close to home. It's like a ten minute drive.

INDIA. Did he used to be really good?

GORDO. Yes. No. I don't know.

INDIA. But you just said –

GORDO. I take it back. I don't know. He got a tennis scholarship but then he didn't take it. Stop asking me so
many questions. Okay?

INDIA. I was just curious –

GORDO. Why – Do you want to have sex with him?

INDIA. Why would you think I want to have sex with him?

GORDO. Because you're both lonely. Or confused. I don't
know. Chaz has never been with a girl before.

INDIA. Why not?

GORDO. I'm thinking maybe he has scabies.

INDIA. He probably just hasn't met the right person yet.

GORDO. Maybe.

(beat)

I have a girlfriend.

INDIA. You do?

GORDO. Uh huh. Her name is Ivy. She's really hot.

INDIA. That's wonderful.

GORDO. It is. Wonderful. She's wonderful.

INDIA. Where did you meet her?

GORDO. …Wal-Mart.

INDIA. Wal-Mart?

GORDO. Uh huh.

INDIA. Well, I hope I get to meet her sometime.

GORDO. We'll see. She's pretty intimidating. You might be
too intimidated by her.

(beat)

I destroyed the entire "Family Movies" aisle at Blockbuster Video. Two weeks ago. The entire genre
– CRASH. Right there on the floor. Cartoons. Disney

classics. That one with Robin Williams…All lying in one big heap on the floor with me right there in the middle. I remember – there was this one girl, a red-head, one of those dopey looking kids with really thick glasses, standing there, next to her mother, just staring at me. Like I was some sort of car crash on the highway. They told me I had to leave Blockbuster after that. They said I was a "danger to myself and to other people. " It was pretty rough.

(GORDO suddenly bangs his head against the desk.)

Why did I do that? Why? Why?

(Does it again. Does it a few times.)

INDIA. Oh my god – Stop!

(GORDO stops.)

GORDO. I'm such an idiot.

INDIA. You're not an idiot.

GORDO. I am. I don't know how to behave like a normal person.

INDIA. Should I…call someone?

GORDO. No.

INDIA. Can I get you something? Water? Do you take Adderall or something?

GORDO. No. I need more discipline.

INDIA. Oh. Okay.

GORDO. Can you tell me to go sit in Time-out?

INDIA. Time-out?

GORDO. Just say. Gordo – Time. Out.

INDIA. Just say it?

GORDO. Now!

INDIA. Okay. Uh…Gordo. Time-out.

GORDO. NO!

INDIA. What?

GORDO. I DON'T WANT TO!

INDIA. *(confused)* But –

(**GORDO** *grabs* **INDIA**'s *wrist. It's a bit scary.*)

INDIA. I…I really think you should go sit in time out.

(*They stand like this for another moment.*)

GORDO. Fine.

(**GORDO** *releases her wrist goes over to the chair in the corner.*)

GORDO. How long?

INDIA. Uh…

GORDO. One minute?

INDIA. Sure. One minute.

(**GORDO** *sits in time-out.* **INDIA** *waits. After about ten seconds,* **GORDO** *stands up.*)

GORDO. Better. See?

(**INDIA** *stands there, frozen.*)

What were we talking about? The Y? Did I tell you about my friend there? Kip.

(*no response*)

Hey.

(*no response*)

Hey, India. Did I tell you about Kip?

(*A moment –* **INDIA** *is a bit fazed.*)

INDIA. You'll uh…let me know when Chaz gets back?

GORDO. What?

INDIA. I'm sorry. I don't think I should be here right now.

GORDO. Why not?

INDIA. What you just did – it's awkward now. You'll tell me when he's back?

(**INDIA** *moves to go. Beat.*)

GORDO. He's back.

INDIA. What?

GORDO. I heard his car pull into the drive-way. About a minute ago. I just didn't tell you.

INDIA. If you're just messing with me…

GORDO. Count to ten and I bet he'll be here.

(Beat. Enter **CHAZ***, carrying a tennis racket and a box of Dunkin Donuts.)*

GORDO. See?

CHAZ. Hey.

*(***CHAZ*** holds up the box.)*

Donuts!

GORDO. Since when do you buy donuts?

CHAZ. I don't know. I was in a good mood this morning. I woke up and I thought to myself – I should buy something. Celebrate.

GORDO. Celebrate what?

CHAZ. Us. India. Our new little humble household.

INDIA. Oh, I –

CHAZ. No, come on. You're one of the family now. One of the Flynns.

INDIA. Okay. Thanks.

CHAZ. We're rolling out the red carpet –

GORDO. With donuts.

CHAZ. Yes. With donuts. All kinds except for coconut, because I know you hate the texture Gordo. Oh – and I was thinking we could all go out for dinner tonight. Somewhere in town. I thought that might be nice. Maybe Chinese.

GORDO. We never go out for dinner.

CHAZ. Which is why I'm suggesting it now. India – do you like Chinese? I didn't even ask.

INDIA. Sure.

CHAZ. General Tsao's Chicken – is that Chinese? I used to love that stuff. I don't know why we never think to get it anymore. It's so good, right? That sauce. It's settled then. Tonight – General Tsao. Tomorrow – who knows, right? *(to* **GORDO***)* How's the arm?

GORDO. Hurts.

CHAZ. I got you Tylenol.

GORDO. Too late. Damage is already done.

CHAZ. It's PM. It'll help you sleep.

GORDO. I'm a broken toy on Christmas morning. Nobody wants to play with me. India tried. But she gave up half-way through. She said she can't stand being around me.

INDIA. I didn't say that.

CHAZ. Wait – what happened?

INDIA. Nothing; it's fine.

GORDO. She gave me a time-out. Ask her.

CHAZ. You gave him a time-out?

INDIA. Yeah…but, he told me to.

CHAZ. *(hard)* You shouldn't do that.

INDIA. He asked for it.

CHAZ. I'm the only one who can say that to him.

INDIA. Okay.

CHAZ. Just me. No one else.

INDIA. I'm sorry. I didn't know.

CHAZ. You're not his parent, okay? He can't have everyone just screaming things at him.

INDIA. I said okay.

(a slight pause)

CHAZ. *(to INDIA)* I'm sorry. It's delicate.

GORDO. What about me? You should apologize to me, too.

CHAZ. I'm sorry. To everyone.

(CHAZ tosses him the bottle.)

CHAZ. Here.

(GORDO struggles to open it.)

CHAZ. It'll be much easer if you ditch the sling.

GORDO. I just made it this morning.

CHAZ. I know.

(pause)

GORDO. Yeah, okay.

(**GORDO** *takes off the sling. Takes a pill.*)

CHAZ. So…

INDIA. So…

CHAZ. So…I taught this kid today.

INDIA. Right. Gordo was telling me you teach tennis.

CHAZ. Uh huh. Jeremy – he's on Sundays. Real cute. Maybe nine. Ten, tops. Totally deaf. Like – nothing. And he does this thing. Okay – so basically he plays every single shot from the baseline. Like even if the ball drops three inches from the net, he just stands there and waits for it. Literally, I'd drop it right over the net just to see if he'd budge, and guess what, he doesn't. He just stands there. Staring at the ball – like it's a UFO coming down to abduct him. And by the time the ball finally does bounce on over, it's basically dribbling on the ground. He would be better off *kick*ing it back to me. I kept wanting to scream MOVE! MOVE JEREMY! JUST MOVE YOUR LITTLE FEET! But. You know. Wouldn't exactly work. *(pause)* So that was my morning…

INDIA. Actually. I think it's really noble what you're doing.

CHAZ. It's just the Y – they create all those programs.

INDIA. Yeah. But not a lot of people would go do that with their time.

(**CHAZ** *shrugs dismissively.*)

(*Throughout the following conversation,* **GORDO**, *feeling a bit left out, slowly gravitates to the window.*)

CHAZ. It can be pretty frustrating actually. Working with people you can't always fully connect with.

INDIA. Me – I couldn't do it. I'd probably just give up after the first day.

CHAZ. You get used to it. It's like training for a marathon – you have to build up stamina.

INDIA. Well – you're pretty good at it.

CHAZ. Good at what?

INDIA. Connecting with people.

GORDO. *(looking out the window)* Holy…shit.

CHAZ. What?

GORDO. Chaz – you have to come see this.

CHAZ. What is it?

GORDO. Come here.

CHAZ. Tell me.

GORDO. Come and look.

(**CHAZ** *goes over to the window.*)

CHAZ. Oh, the car.

GORDO. You knew about it?

CHAZ. I saw it when I came in.

GORDO. You don't think that's weird?

CHAZ. I guess.

GORDO. It's just sitting there.

CHAZ. It's probably waiting for someone. One of our neighbors.

GORDO. What is that? A mercedes?

CHAZ. Bentley, I think.

GORDO. It's watching us.

CHAZ. I wouldn't worry too much about it.

(**GORDO** *paces a bit.*)

INDIA. Did you see anyone. In the car?

CHAZ. Nah. Windows are tinted.

(**GORDO** *stops pacing.*)

GORDO. OH MY GOD. Chaz. You know who it is?

CHAZ. Who?

GORDO. You know who.

CHAZ. No.

GORDO. Yeah. Uh huh.

CHAZ. I don't know what you're talking about.

GORDO. Three words:

*(**CHAZ** thinks a moment.)*

CHAZ. It's not Child Protective Services.

GORDO. Yeah man.

CHAZ. No way.

GORDO. They finally came. After all these years. Like we always talked about.

CHAZ. Why would they just be sitting out there?

GORDO. They're spying on us. Taking footage. Collecting evidence.

CHAZ. I don't think government officials drive around in Bentleys.

GORDO. Bill Gates – he gives money to them. The Gates Foundation.

CHAZ. What?

GORDO. He gives money to everyone. Oh my god. I'm going to get dragged off to the asylum by Bill Gates himself. Holy shit.

CHAZ. *(to **INDIA**)* You okay?

INDIA. Uh huh.

CHAZ. *(to **INDIA**)* Sorry about before.

INDIA. It's fine.

CHAZ. I should have given you a heads up.

INDIA. It's fine, really.

GORDO. Wait – Chaz – Did you do this? Did you call them up?

CHAZ. What are you talking about?

GORDO. You did. Didn't you.

CHAZ. I didn't call anyone, Gordo.

GORDO. Adopt India, get rid of me. The symmetry. It's beautiful.

CHAZ. You need to relax dude. Take a deep breath.

GORDO. "What ominous black car outside? I didn't notice anything."

CHAZ. I have no idea what you're talking about.

GORDO. Bullshit.

CHAZ. Enough with the cursing already.

GORDO. Fuck. Shit. Motherfucker shit-pants ass-face.

CHAZ. You're disgusting. Why don't you take a walk.

GORDO. What? So you and India can talk about me? Talk about how messed up I am?

CHAZ. You're out of control.

GORDO. Yeah?

CHAZ. Yeah.

GORDO. I'll show you out of control. Just remember – you brought this one upon yourself.

CHAZ. Brought what?

(**GORDO** *stares at him. Storms out. A brief pause.*)

India –

INDIA. Yeah.

CHAZ. Hide. Now.

INDIA. What?

CHAZ. Go. Duck under my desk.

INDIA. Uh – okay.

(**INDIA** *ducks under the desk.*)

(**GORDO** *returns with the football helmet.*)

CHAZ. Gordo –

(**GORDO** *stands there.*)

I'm trying to help you.

(**GORDO** *stares at him.*)

CHAZ. What else am I supposed to do! Tell me. You can't keep doing this.

GORDO. One.

CHAZ. Really. I'm running out of options.

GORDO. Two.

CHAZ. You have to start listening to me.

GORDO. Three!

(**GORDO** *charges.*)

CHAZ. Ah!

(**GORDO** *hits* **CHAZ** *in the legs. They both fall to the ground.*)

GORDO. NO LEGS! NO MORE LEGS FOR YOU!

CHAZ. Stop it! Stop!

(*They struggle.*)

GORDO. AGGGHHHH!!!

CHAZ. Get off! NOW.

(*The doorbell rings.* **CHAZ** *and* **GORDO** *look up.*)

(*The doorbell rings again.*)

GORDO. They're here. Say goodbye. This is last you'll ever see of me.

CHAZ. I'm not saying anything –

GORDO. Don't try to visit.

CHAZ. Visit where?

GORDO. You know.

CHAZ. I DIDN'T FUCKING CALL ANYONE!

(*The doorbell rings again.*)

(*This time,* **INDIA** *scuttles out from beneath the desk. Without looking at either of them, she exits offstage.*)

(*The sound of a door opening and then closing.*)

(*Enter* **INDIA**, *followed by* **OSCAR**, *50s. He wears a cashmere sport coat over a golf shirt and jeans.*)

(**OSCAR** *looks at* **CHAZ** *and* **GORDO** *on the ground, confused. They stare back, also confused.*)

(**INDIA** *glares at* **OSCAR**.)

INDIA. AGGHHH!!!

(**INDIA** *storms off.*)

(*The sound of a door slamming.*)

(*Blackout.*)

End of Act I

ACT II

4.

(A few minutes later. **GORDO** *sits on the couch, a bit frazzled, staring at the football helmet on his lap.* **CHAZ** *hovers nearby. After a moment.)*

(Offstage, pounding on door.)

OSCAR. INDIA! INDIA!

(Enter **OSCAR** *from the direction of the pounding.)*

CHAZ. Was there a lot of traffic?

OSCAR. Traffic? No.

CHAZ. That's the worst. Sitting there. Just – waiting.

*(***OSCAR** *checks his watch. Then digs into his pockets and pulls out an unopened pack of cigarettes. He holds the pack uneasily.)*

OSCAR. Would it be alright –

*(***GORDO***'s eyes open wide.)*

GORDO. Chaz –

CHAZ. Uh –

GORDO. Tell him.

CHAZ. We don't – I'm sorry.

GORDO. This is a strictly non-smoking zone.

OSCAR. Oh, of course.

CHAZ. You understand.

OSCAR. No. You're right, it's a disgusting habit. That's why I quit in the first place.

*(***OSCAR** *puts the pack back in his jacket pocket.)*

OSCAR. How long has she been in there?

CHAZ. A few minutes maybe?

OSCAR. And there's no master key? No special trick to the locks in this house?

CHAZ. Maybe she'll come out…if you ask her nicely.

OSCAR. No. Not my daughter. She's very stubborn. She gets that from me.

CHAZ. I take it she wasn't expecting you then?

OSCAR. Oh…she was expecting me.

CHAZ. She seems a bit reluctant to see you.

OSCAR. No…trust me, she wanted all of this to happen. That's what you need to understand about India. She's calculated this exact scenario. Me driving however many miles just to have a door slammed in my face. Sitting here incapacitated while she – I don't know. She's probably watching TV – that's what she's probably doing. She's probably laughing her ass off watching some idiotic reality show on MTV!

(Beat)

GORDO. We don't have a TV.

OSCAR. Mind if I take a seat?

CHAZ. Please.

(OSCAR sits down on the couch next to GORDO.)

GORDO. Nice jacket.

OSCAR. Thank you.

GORDO. Can I touch it?

OSCAR. Go ahead.

(GORDO touches it.)

GORDO. Feels expensive.

OSCAR. My wife got it for me.

GORDO. Feels like someone ripped it straight off the back of a Himalayan mountain goat.

(GORDO sniffs the jacket.)

OSCAR. What are you doing?

GORDO. Nothing.

(**OSCAR** *takes his arm back. Stands up.*)

OSCAR. So what, you boys just out of school?

CHAZ. Us? No.

OSCAR. Your place. It has that feel.

CHAZ. We grew up here. There used to be more stuff.

OSCAR. I lived in filth after I graduated. A dingy apartment under a bridge. With three guys and a parakeet.

(*noticing*)

Why do you have so many telephone books?

CHAZ. It's a hobby. We collect them.

OSCAR. Odd thing to collect.

CHAZ. It's this project we're working on.

GORDO. Chaz's project. He's on a quest.

CHAZ. I'm sorry, I'm just a little confused. So she still lives with you?

OSCAR. India?

CHAZ. Yeah.

OSCAR. Of course she lives with me. Where else would she live?

CHAZ. I don't know. I just find it strange that she would go looking for a room if she's got a nice place to stay.

OSCAR. Right?

(*calling out*)

Did you hear that India? This man says he doesn't understand why anyone would run away from such a nice family!

(*They all listen for a response. Nothing.*)

IF YOU COME OUT RIGHT NOW I WILL NOT GET ANGRY! THERE WILL BE NO CONSEQUENCES – WE CAN JUST GET IN THE CAR AND GO HOME.

(*nothing*)

India?

(nothing)

FINE. I'M JUST GOING TO SIT HERE AND HANG
OUT WITH YOUR NEW FRIENDS! I HOPE THAT'S
ALRIGHT WITH YOU!

OSCAR. See what I'm dealing with?

(pause)

GORDO. She probably just hates you.

OSCAR. Excuse me?

GORDO. She probably just, hates you.

OSCAR. Hate is a very strong word, son.

GORDO. She blames you.

OSCAR. For what?

GORDO. For having all this extra anger.

OSCAR. She's angry at me?

GORDO. She's got lots and lots of anger. She carries it
around with her like a cape on her back. Like a big
heavy cape.

OSCAR. Did she say that? Has she said that to you?

GORDO. No. But I know.

OSCAR. I don't understand.

GORDO. It's pretty obvious.

OSCAR. *(to* **CHAZ***)* What is? What is he talking about?

CHAZ. He's just talking to talk.

GORDO. No. She hates him. She's paralyzed by it. It's like a
poison from a rare African spider.

OSCAR. You better start thinking about the words coming
out of your mouth. Because what you're saying young
man, it could be interpreted as pretty damn offensive.

GORDO. I'm a prophet – I speak only the truth.

OSCAR. Yeah, now you're just making a bunch of noise.

GORDO. I've come down from the Mount to speak with all
the little people.

OSCAR. I think you're mixed up, son. I think you're very
mixed up right now.

CHAZ. He's right – you're not making any sense.

GORDO. I make sense. Ask India – she gets me.

OSCAR. India?

GORDO. We're like the same person.

OSCAR. You are *nothing* like my daughter.

GORDO. Wrong. We both like Bingo.

OSCAR. You are nothing like her. You are rude. And… and…immature.

GORDO. What about her?

OSCAR. India. She's – I don't know. Misguided.

GORDO. I'm misguided!

CHAZ. *(re: the helmet)* Gordo – why don't you go put that back in your room.

GORDO. I don't want to.

CHAZ. So you don't lose it.

GORDO. I'm not going to lose it.

CHAZ. Please. I really need you to go put that away. I really need that right now.

(**GORDO** *looks at* **CHAZ**. *Sees the desperation on his face.*)

GORDO. Okay.

(**GORDO** *exits with the helmet.*)

OSCAR. Jesus – that kid.

CHAZ. I know.

OSCAR. He's going to get himself in a lot of trouble some-day.

CHAZ. I know.

OSCAR. You can't just say those kinds of things. Not in front of strangers. I could have been what – someone with a really bad temper? Knocked his front teeth right out.

CHAZ. Yeah.

OSCAR. Is he like that all the time?

CHAZ. No. He's – well…Not all the time. Just sometimes. More so lately I guess. Maybe it's some kind of phase.

OSCAR. If he were my child, I wouldn't let him talk like that. Not in a million years.

*(**OSCAR** checks his watch. Exits offstage.)*

OSCAR. INDIA!

*(**OSCAR** bangs on the door.)*

INDIA!

(He returns.)

CHAZ. What would you do? If you were – his parent.

OSCAR. I'd let him know that that was unacceptable, end of story. I wouldn't tolerate it. Not like that. No way.

CHAZ. Yeah. Yeah.

(pause)

Can I ask you a kind of weird question?

OSCAR. What do you want to ask me?

CHAZ. I know India means a lot to you –

OSCAR. She's my daughter.

CHAZ. Right. Exactly. So I guess what I'm wondering is if you came here to get her because you thought you had to or if maybe it was something else.

OSCAR. Something more like what?

CHAZ. I don't know. It's a stupid question.

OSCAR. What did you mean by *because I thought I had to*?

CHAZ. Because – you have no choice?

OSCAR. Look kid. It's pretty simple. My daughter takes a giant side-step from reality and its my job to reel her back in. It's not exactly rocket science.

CHAZ. Right, sure.

OSCAR. You'll understand one day.

CHAZ. I don't know.

OSCAR. You will. When you have your own family.

CHAZ. We'll see.

OSCAR. Come on, didn't one of you boys ever act out at some point? Try to run away?

CHAZ. Us? No.

OSCAR. I did. Run away.

CHAZ. Really?

OSCAR. Sure. But it was different. What India is doing is – well, it's different. Me – it was what everybody did. It was part of the times.

CHAZ. Where'd you go?

OSCAR. Carmel Valley. The northwestern corner of San Diego.

CHAZ. Our mom is from California.

OSCAR. Oh yeah? Whereabouts?

CHAZ. We don't know. We think she was a "hippie" though. We once found an old photograph of her with flowers in her hair.

OSCAR. Why don't you ask her?

CHAZ. She's, uh – she's not really a part of lives anymore.

OSCAR. I'm sorry to hear that.

CHAZ. It's fine. We're – fine now.

OSCAR. It's a beautiful state. California. Beautiful people. Great wine.

CHAZ. And so what – you just packed up one day and moved out there?

OSCAR. Something like that. Me and a few guys, we convinced this friend of ours to steal his parents station wagon and drive us to this commune we had read about in a magazine. Summer of 1965, the summer before my senior year in high school.

CHAZ. And what about your parents? They must have been pretty pissed.

OSCAR. Oh they were. I was supposed to be working for my uncle that summer. Selling sporting equipment – jock straps and whatnot.

CHAZ. I think I could sell equipment.

OSCAR. You looking for a job?

CHAZ. An opportunity. Some sort of change I guess.

OSCAR. You and I, we should talk. I run a whole string of them now – sporting good stores. Expanded my uncle's shop across all five boroughs. We're always looking for young, energetic kids.

CHAZ. In the city?

OSCAR. Eight stops on Metro-North, it's an easy commute.

CHAZ. And – the pay?

OSCAR. What about it?

CHAZ. Is it – um, livable?

(OSCAR eyes him, confused at the question.)

OSCAR. You got to work your way up. That's how these things work. Start behind the counter for a few months and see what happens. Maybe you'll hate it, I don't know. I'll give you my number, how's that?

CHAZ. Are you sure?

OSCAR. It's no big deal. I do this kind of thing all the time. Plus, this could be a sort of token. For your hospitality. Here. Take a card.

(OSCAR hands CHAZ a business card.)

You give me a call when you're ready to talk.

(GORDO returns, sans helmet. He stands in the doorway.)

GORDO. Hi.

OSCAR. Gordon – that's your name, right?

(GORDO nods.)

OSCAR. Gordon. I need to know if you're ready to start behaving like an adult.

GORDO. *(unconvincing)* Okay.

OSCAR. No. Not okay. I'm asking you.

GORDO. I'm ready.

OSCAR. One more outburst like that and that's it. There will be serious consequences.

GORDO. I put the helmet away.

OSCAR. Look at me.

GORDO. I said okay.

OSCAR. *(very firm)* I said look at me.

(He does. **OSCAR** *stares back.)*

OSCAR. *(firm)* I'm serious.

(beat)

CHAZ. India's dad, Mr –

OSCAR. Waterman.

CHAZ. Mr. Waterman was just telling me about this time
when he ran away. Do you want to hear about it?

GORDO. He ran away?

CHAZ. He went to California.

GORDO. Did he go to Disneyland?

CHAZ. He went to a commune actually.

GORDO. What – like a cult?

OSCAR. No. Like a commune.

GORDO. And?

OSCAR. And so I ran away. I wasn't always just some suit and
tie, you know. I got my fair share of stories.

*(***GORDO*** *goes back to his seat on the couch.)*

I was telling your brother – it's not like how it is with
India. Our parents – they were from a very different
world than us. My dad used to sit up listening to Jackie
Gleason albums and Gordon Jenkins. He was I guess
what you'd call "square." I never really talked to him.
But India – me and India, it's not the same thing. She
knows she can talk to me. We shouldn't be having this
sort of misunderstanding in the first place. I'm a very
reasonable man. We should be able to reason with one
another.

GORDO. What'd you do there? At the commune.

OSCAR. Oh, man.

GORDO. Did you run around naked all the time?

OSCAR. No.

(beat)

Just try to imagine that for a second. The rush. Kids from all over the country looking for some kind of escape, retreating from the terrible violence and confusion of the world around them. Driving their parents cars and carrying nothing but the clothes on their backs.

CHAZ. Sounds like such a release.

OSCAR. Yeah...But it's funny. Hearing myself talk about it like this – like I had it all figured out back then. The reality of it was a very different thing. That place, the so-called commune, it was really just a run-down building in the middle of nowhere. An old abandoned shotgun-shell manufacturing plant left over from World War II. We pretty just sat around all day smoking dope and eating potato salad out of little plastic cups. Not really doing anything in particular, just kind of sitting around waiting for something to happen. And of course there was no running water. No toilets. No medical facilities. A lot of kids got hurt and had to leave. We weren't getting the riff raff just yet, people with missing teeth and things like that, but it wasn't exactly the Garden of Eden we went there expecting it to be.

CHAZ. So that's it?

OSCAR. Pretty much.

CHAZ. Sounds a lot like this.

OSCAR. How's that?

CHAZ. A bunch of people waiting around for something to happen.

OSCAR. Ha. That's very clever. Very funny.

(checks his watch)

Jesus. Long day, eh?

(plops down)

I'm exhausted. I am. I am sick and tired of having to wait for my own daughter to grow up and think about someone else for a change.

(A moment.)

(**GORDO** *scootches next to* **OSCAR**. *He very slowly and very gently rests his head on his shoulder.*)

OSCAR. You tired too, son?

GORDO. A little.

OSCAR. I hear you. I hear you.

(Enter **INDIA**, *fuming.* **GORDO** *lifts his head as soon as he sees her.)*

INDIA. God you're such a cliché. Telling stories about your outlaw days in the sixties.

OSCAR. Are you ready to come back now?

INDIA. No.

OSCAR. There's a sandwich from Balducci's in the car for you.

INDIA. I'm not hungry.

OSCAR. India – get in the car.

INDIA. No.

OSCAR. I said get in the car.

INDIA. No.

INDIA. This isn't a discussion – I'm telling you to get your things and come outside.

INDIA. I'm not coming.

OSCAR. Do you want me to make a scene? Throw you over my shoulder like a toddler and carry you out?

INDIA. Go ahead.

*(***OSCAR** *doesn't budge.)*

OSCAR. India – I did what you wanted. I came all the way out here. Now it's your turn to make a few concessions.

INDIA. I said I'm not coming with you.

OSCAR. You left the address sitting right out in the open. Obviously you wanted me to come to this place.

INDIA. No, I didn't.

OSCAR. It was right there. On your bed-stand.

INDIA. That was an accident.

OSCAR. Do you have even the remotest idea of how scary that is? Waking up to find out that your child has gone missing? Thinking she might be passed out in some drug lord's bathtub in Queens?

(**INDIA** *shrugs.*)

OSCAR. Right. Of course. It's all just *whatever.*

(*a moment*)

You know – Mom was too angry to come. She wanted to call the police and have you stay in a jail cell overnight. Figured that might teach you a lesson. I at least convinced her to let me come instead.

INDIA. Thanks.

OSCAR. Jesus India. I'm really trying here.

INDIA. It's not about you.

OSCAR. Then what is this about?

INDIA. I don't know.

OSCAR. I think you do.

INDIA. Nope. Sorry.

OSCAR. I think you have something you need to tell me.

INDIA. I already said I don't have anything to say.

(**OSCAR** *gives her a look.*)

INDIA. What?

OSCAR. Come on.

(**INDIA** *doesn't respond.*)

Regarding…something you've taken?

(*no response*)

Something that belongs to me?

(*no response*)

Something that is my personal property.

(*no response*)

India.

(*no response*)

India.

(a long silence)

Where's Bob?

INDIA. Bob who?

OSCAR. *(slowly, deliberately)* Where. Is. Bob?

CHAZ. Who's Bob?

INDIA. I don't know anyone by that name.

OSCAR. You both just disappear – on exactly the same day? I find that hard to believe.

INDIA. Doesn't seem so unbelievable to me.

OSCAR. India –

INDIA. Maybe my leaving opened the door for him. Or maybe he finally jumped out the window. It's only three flights up. He might have actually made it.

CHAZ. Who's Bob?

OSCAR. You've hidden him. You've locked him in a closet.

INDIA. Check all the closets.

OSCAR. The garage maybe. Or one of the bathtubs.

GORDO. What's in our bathtub?

INDIA. Nothing. Go check for yourself.

OSCAR. It would be a lot easier if you would just tell me where he is.

INDIA. Maybe you should check the toilets then. And the oven. You should definitely check the oven.

OSCAR. Okay. You want me to look around? I'll look around.

*(**OSCAR** storms off to the bedrooms.)*

CHAZ. What is it that he's looking for?

INDIA. Beats me.

*(**OSCAR** returns carrying **INDIA**'s French horn case.)*

OSCAR. Look what I found!

INDIA. So?

OSCAR. You haven't played the horn since fifth grade.

(**OSCAR** *sets the case down. Opens it up. It's empty.*)

INDIA. Oooo…Scary.

(**OSCAR** *sniffs the case.*)

OSCAR. It smells like him.

(**OSCAR** *puts his hand into his coat pocket and pulls out a handful of loose pet food – small pellets. Holds it out. Crawls around the room.*)

OSCAR. Here Bob. Here.

(**OSCAR** *makes a clicking sound with his tongue.*)

Daddy's got some food for you. Some foodie woodie.

INDIA. You make it like he can actually understand what you're saying.

OSCAR. So he *is* here?

INDIA. I didn't say that.

OSCAR. He is. I smelled him. I can smell him.

(**OSCAR** *makes more clicking sounds.*)

Here boy. Here.

INDIA. OH MY GOD. This is so embarrassing. Stop!

(**OSCAR** *gets up from the ground.*)

OSCAR. You're right. It is. Embarrassing. Having to beg my own daughter to give me back something that is mine. Something that obviously has a lot of meaning to me!

(*Pause. Takes a deep breath.*)

But if you tell me he's not here, he's not here. Right? I have to be able to trust you. Now, and in the future. I'm your family, India. I'm not going anywhere. Whether you like it or not. (*beat*) So? Which is it?

(*pause*)

Is he here or not?

INDIA. He's not here.

OSCAR. Is that your answer?

INDIA. …Yes.

OSCAR. You're sure?

INDIA. Yes.

OSCAR. You're *sure.*

INDIA. *(averting eye contact)* Yes.

(a slight pause.)

OSCAR. Well okay. If that's what you're telling me. But how about this. Let's say I give you a bit more time to think about it – to think over your answer – and then we'll try this again.

INDIA. You're going to leave?

OSCAR. How much more time do you think you need? A day? A week?

INDIA. Seriously?

OSCAR. I'll give you a day, how's that? That seems fair.

INDIA. You're just going to let me stay here?

OSCAR. You're a big girl. You need to start making your own decisions. I'll come back tomorrow. After lunch.

INDIA. …Okay.

OSCAR. Just one day though. That's all.

(beat)

OSCAR. Chaz. Gordon. Very nice to meet you.

CHAZ. Nice to meet you too Sir. Really.

OSCAR. Take good care of my daughter.

CHAZ. We'll do our best.

OSCAR. India – I'll see you soon.

INDIA. Bye.

*(**OSCAR** heads to the door.)*

OSCAR. Think about everything we talked about. About what it means to be a family.

INDIA. I heard you.

*(**OSCAR** goes over to **INDIA** – kisses her on the forehead. Exits.)*

(INDIA stands as the lights fade.)

5.

*(Later that day. **INDIA** sits alone on the couch holding her French horn case on her lap. Looks around to make sure no one's there. Opens the case, slowly. Pulls out... a rabbit. Live. Docile. Really cute. Well, cute enough to elicit some oohs and ahs but not enough to upstage the actors. The kind you'd want to take pictures with at a petting zoo. With a collar.)*

INDIA. You better not pee on me.

(holds him up in the air)

Sorry for stuffing you in a sock drawer – that was just temporary. So Dad wouldn't find you.

(They stare at one another a moment.)

Yeah...I know. You don't like me either. It's okay. We don't actually have to like each other. God, who would even think to shackle a rabbit? Yeah. No need to answer. We both know who.

*(Enter **CHAZ**. **INDIA** quickly stashes Bob back in the [perforated somehow] music case. She rushes offstage to get rid of it.)*

(On her way out) I'm not leaving tomorrow.

CHAZ. *(calling after **INDIA**)* Your Dad seems to think you are! It's funny you never mentioned him before. Or that you still happen to live with him.

*(**INDIA** re-enters.)*

You're not really twenty-four, are you?

INDIA. No.

CHAZ. How old are you?

(beat)

INDIA. Eighteen.

CHAZ. Right.

INDIA. I'm legal.

CHAZ. You're in *high* school.

INDIA. Yeah? So.

CHAZ. So – it's a problem.

INDIA. Not really.

CHAZ. You...should go back. Finish your classes.

INDIA. But you heard my Dad – he said he was fine with me being here.

CHAZ. That's not the point. It's a big decision. Probably the wrong decision. I can't be responsible for you deciding something like that.

INDIA. You're not – I'm the one making the decision.

CHAZ. You're too young. You don't have enough – perspective.

INDIA. What are you – like five minutes older than me?

CHAZ. I have a bit more experience than you do.

INDIA. In what – living like a hobbit?

CHAZ. In living out certain consequences.

INDIA. God, you sound like my Dad. Consequences, responsibility. Bla bla bla.

(pause)

You know what's so frustrating? Everyone keeps telling me I can't do things because I'm *soo* young. I'm *soo* naïve. I'm so inexperienced. Bullshit. So many famous people did so many cool, revolutionary things when they were young. Mozart. Orson Welles. Bob Dylan ran away three times. He even joined the circus.

CHAZ. It's not like I want to do this. Throw you out.

INDIA. So don't.

CHAZ. You're really nice to have around. To talk to. And to share stuff with.

INDIA. But...

CHAZ. But school is really important. It's where you set up your whole future.

INDIA. Look at you – You didn't even graduate.

CHAZ. I went to high school.

INDIA. And what about college?

CHAZ. College isn't for everyone.

INDIA. Gordo said you got some sort of tennis scholarship.

CHAZ. Yeah. So?

INDIA. So – If you're so *pro* academia, why didn't you take it?

CHAZ. I did take it.

INDIA. I don't understand.

CHAZ. I took it. I went.

INDIA. So what happened?

CHAZ. I went. It was okay. I took some classes. Played on the team. And then I left.

INDIA. Why'd you leave?

CHAZ. It's complicated. Gordo was having a hard time. I took a term off. One off term turned into two, into three, and so on.

INDIA. That sucks.

CHAZ. No – it was my choice. I made the call. It was the right thing to do.

(pause)

INDIA. So where should I go now?

CHAZ. You have a pretty nice home, it sounds like.

INDIA. Ew. No.

CHAZ. And a family.

INDIA. Are you kidding? You met my dad.

CHAZ. He seemed pretty nice to me.

INDIA. He's a bourgeois lump of boringness. Ugh. I wish I had been left in a cardboard box on some desert highway. You guys are so lucky, you have no idea.

CHAZ. Don't say that.

INDIA. I mean it. You guys got a blank check handed to you. Someone gave you a fucking blank check. And what? You've just been sitting here in this room, wallowing.

CHAZ. Hey.

INDIA. Sorry. But It's true. You're obsessed. Your brain is like a haunted house.

CHAZ. We've been through a lot, me and Gordo.

INDIA. I know. But so have a lot of people, right?

CHAZ. We were left in a parking lot. Think about that. A parking lot. Our parents drove us there one morning and just never came back. All they left us with is a house full of stuff. That was like our consolation prize – all their stuff.

INDIA. So – you got a lot of stuff. That's cool at least.

CHAZ. We've mostly sold it all by now. Furniture, my mom's jewelry collection, the TV.

INDIA. Why not the house?

CHAZ. You mean sell the house?

INDIA. Yeah. Why not?

CHAZ. What do you mean?

INDIA. Why do you still live here?

CHAZ. It's our *house*. It's where we live.

INDIA. Do you think they're still coming back for you? Is that why?

(a pause)

(CHAZ *goes over to the mail carrier and takes out a handful of letters. Hw hands the stack to* **INDIA.** *She looks at the top envelope.)*

INDIA. Mr. and Mrs. Norman J. Flynn. 1070 Taramac Trail. Englewood, Colorado.

GORDO. Only eight Flynns in all of Englewood.

(INDIA *flips through the other envelopes.)*

INDIA. Dr. Margaret Flynn. 3 Quintree Lane.

CHAZ. I'm thinking maybe a step-aunt or a third cousin moved out to Colorado sometime in the nineties, and they're just sitting on their porch, whittling a bar of soap, waiting to receive a letter about their forgotten family back on the east coast.

INDIA. You write to all these people?

CHAZ. Uh huh.

INDIA. What do you say?

CHAZ. Hi. How's it going. Are you related to me?

INDIA. Seriously?

CHAZ. It's more formal than that.

INDIA. And so what – you need to stay here until you get a response?

CHAZ. *(suddenly embarrassed)* I don't know. It's silly. It's just – something I do.

(**CHAZ** *puts the letters back in the box.*)

(**INDIA** *watches in silence.*)

INDIA. Come with me.

CHAZ. Where?

INDIA. I don't know. California.

CHAZ. What's in California?

INDIA. Something. I don't know. I think I'm supposed to go there.

CHAZ. Not everyone can just up and leave their family like that.

INDIA. Gordo's not your family. He's a pain in the ass.

CHAZ. He's my responsibility.

INDIA. Is there something actually wrong with him? Like seriously actually wrong? He seems pretty smart.

CHAZ. I don't know. I don't think so. I mean, everyone has something wrong with them, right? It's a sliding scale?

INDIA. I'm pretty messed up, but I'm not like running into walls or anything.

CHAZ. Yeah…

INDIA. And he's got his girlfriend, right? Ivy?

CHAZ. He told you about her?

INDIA. Yeah. He said she was "wonderful."

(beat)

CHAZ. Ivy is a character from Soul Caliber. It's a video game. They have it at Wal-Mart. He plays it on this consol they have there.

INDIA. He said…she would intimidate me.

CHAZ. That's because she has a sword that turns into a whip and can do back flips.

INDIA. Wow.

CHAZ. And she has breasts the size of killer whales.

INDIA. Okay. Now I'm intimidated.

(beat)

INDIA. Seriously. You should come.

CHAZ. I thought you didn't like me.

INDIA. What?

CHAZ. I just got that feeling.

INDIA. I don't even know you.

CHAZ. I thought you just thought I was awkward and like, crushingly boring.

INDIA. I don't think you're boring. I think you're gallant… In an old-fashioned kind of way. How you're always putting other people before yourself – it's just. I don't know anyone like that. You're like a dying breed or whatever. Except, well, it's just that it's weird that no one really notices. Like your brother. Or anyone really. But I do. I mean, notice.

(no response)

And besides – I don't have a license.

CHAZ. A driver's license?

INDIA. I live in Manhattan. No one knows how to drive there.

CHAZ. So you want me for my car.

INDIA. No…

CHAZ. You want me to drive you across the country.

INDIA. I want you to drive yourself across the country, and bring me with you. I'm really fun to travel with. I promise. Like really, really fun. And I'm a master at the radio. I can find radio stations that you never even knew existed. The stations *in between* the stations.

CHAZ. Why are you so intent on me driving there? To California.

INDIA. Because...I don't know. We're like, the same. We're both kinda stuck I guess.

CHAZ. I'm not stuck.

INDIA. You're not exactly living it up.

CHAZ. I could leave.

INDIA. That's what I always said. Back home, sitting on my bed. *I could leave whenever I want; I could just get up and walk out.* And then, about a year ago, I just started doing it. Getting up and leaving right in the middle of things. Like if I was watching a movie and it was absolutely god-awful, I'd just get up and leave. Or if I was having dinner with a bunch of friends and the conversation just sounded like empty white noise gossip talk, I'd just get up and go eat by myself. Because life is short, right? We're all going to die so we might as well do what we want while we're here. That's what all the philosophers tell you. All those dead French guys. And look – they're dead, right? So they must have been onto something. I guess I'm kind of cobbling together my worldview as I go along. Right now I'm in a very dead French guys/James Dean outlaw place. But tomorrow – who knows? Right?

(a slight pause)

INDIA. It's my birthday by the way.

CHAZ. Today?

INDIA. Yesterday, actually. This was my birthday present to myself. Coming here. A sort of Emancipation Proclamation.

CHAZ. Well, Happy Birthday.

INDIA. Thanks.

(silence)

CHAZ. What would we do? In California.

INDIA. You could...go back to school. Right?

CHAZ. No, I'm too old.

INDIA. Yeah, you're a regular Old Man River.

CHAZ. And so what – I'd live with you?

INDIA. Why not?

CHAZ. On a beach in California?

INDIA. We could live on the beach. Or Berkeley. I hear Berkeley's pretty cool.

CHAZ. And – just – live there? Like – people?

(Pause. **INDIA** *looks at* **CHAZ***. He holds her glance for a moment and then looks away.)*

INDIA. I think your subconscious was calling out to me, when you invited me to come live here.

CHAZ. I think you're projecting.

INDIA. That ad you posted? Your commas were basically typographical tear-drops, crying out in desperation.

CHAZ. Now you're just blatantly making stuff up.

(a moment)

INDIA. Okay. Okay. I don't want to force you to do anything. I'm not going to get down on my knees and beg. If you and your car want to come along, then that would be really cool. If not, I would really appreciate it if you could drive me to the train station. I was thinking of leaving tomorrow morning. Early.

CHAZ. Okay.

INDIA. Okay you'll come with me?

CHAZ. Okay I'll drive you to the train station.

INDIA. But you'll at least think about it?

CHAZ. I can't – I'm sorry.

INDIA. Just think about it.

(Enter **GORDO***. Stretches and yawns.)*

GORDO. Best – Nap – Ever.

INDIA. I'm gonna go start packing my things.

(exit **INDIA***)*

(**GORDO** *plops down on the couch. Puts his feet up.*)

GORDO. Wasn't that scary? Back then? When I thought it was you know who at the door?

CHAZ. Uh huh.

GORDO. Oh man. Close call. We've got to come up with some kind of plan in case that ever happens again. Stop, drop, and roll. That sort of thing.

(pause)

CHAZ. She's taking off.

(**GORDO** *sits up.*)

GORDO. India?

CHAZ. Yeah.

GORDO. I knew it. From the minute she walked in, I knew she was trouble.

CHAZ. It's probably better..

GORDO. Right? Oil and vinegar. Cowboys and Indians...

CHAZ. With her situation...

GORDO. She's a dirty homewrecker, that's what she really is.

CHAZ. She needs to go back to school, figure things out.

GORDO. Back to the status quo. Back to the way it should be. Chazzie and Gordo – The Reunion Tour. Tickets on sale now.

(a moment)

CHAZ. Gordo?

GORDO. Hit me, mi hermano.

CHAZ. Do you ever...Do you ever think about that whole day at the parking lot?

GORDO. *Whoa.* Where did that come from?

CHAZ. Just – go with me for a minute.

GORDO. Wow. Okay.

CHAZ. What do you remember?

(a slight pause)

GORDO. Uh. I remember coupons. Lots and lots of coupons, all over the ground where we were sitting. I remember that.

CHAZ. Do you remember what Mom did?

GORDO. Mom?

CHAZ. Before she got in the car.

GORDO. She...I don't know. Tripped over a fire hydrant?

CHAZ. She put your hand in mine.

GORDO. Oh, right.

CHAZ. She didn't say anything. She just gave me your hand.

GORDO. Yeah. I remember that.

(pause)

CHAZ. You used to be pretty good at stuff, remember? You were good at English – you even got that story published in the school literary magazine – the one about me and you in the underwater castle.

GORDO. It was a fortress. Not a castle.

CHAZ. I don't know what happened. It's like I didn't give you the right vitamins.

GORDO. You didn't give me any vitamins.

CHAZ. You might have turned out different, that's all I'm saying.

GORDO. What are you talking about?

CHAZ. Mom and Dad. You would have been different.

GORDO. Yeah – so? I would have become some boring grown-up. I would drink coffee and talk about my taxes all the time. I'm my own person. I'm a force of nature.

CHAZ. But maybe –

GORDO. What?

CHAZ. I don't know.

GORDO. Look at me – I'm fun. I'm the funnest guy on the block.

CHAZ. But...The way you act.

GORDO. That's just me dude. It's who I am.

CHAZ. Right. But –

GORDO. The whole animal kingdom is acting out – remember? I'm just obeying my natural biology.

CHAZ. But I mean – what if I wasn't here? To clean up after you all the time.

GORDO. Why wouldn't you be here?

CHAZ. I might meet someone someday. I might, I don't know, get a job offer.

GORDO. No you wouldn't – don't even joke about that man.

CHAZ. Come on. You must have at least considered that I might not…always be here.

GORDO. Why would I consider that?

CHAZ. I'm just trying to broach the topic. To have a civil conversation with you.

GORDO. Well maybe you should try being a little less *aggressive* about it. Your basically mauling my soul with your so-called civil behavior.

CHAZ. Better than mauling an entire video store.

(**GORDO** *puts his fingers in his ears.*)

CHAZ. What? I have to be able to talk to you about these things with you at some point.

GORDO. *(frantic)* I said I'm sorry, okay!? What else do you want me to say?

(a long pause)

How about I take out the mail? Okay?

CHAZ. It's Sunday.

GORDO. So? Let me do my job. I'm good at that, right?

CHAZ. Fine.

(**GORDO** *picks up the mail container.*)

GORDO. Let's see what we've got this week –

(He looks at the letters inside.)

GORDO. Englewood, Colorado.

CHAZ. Yup.

GORDO. You think we've got relatives all the way out there?

CHAZ. I don't know. Worth a shot.

(pause)

GORDO. It's weird that no one ever responds.

CHAZ. Got to keep trying –

GORDO. Sure, sure. It's just interesting, that's all.

*(**GORDO** heads outside with the mail bin.)*

*(**CHAZ** returns to his desk. Opens up a phone book. Begins typing a letter.)*

*(Enter **GORDO**. Still carrying the mail container.)*

GORDO. Oh my god. Chaz. Oh my god.

*(Enter **INDIA**, frazzled. Carrying Bob in one hand and a plastic bag in the other.)*

INDIA. It's not what you think.

GORDO. Oh my god.

INDIA. You need to stop spazzing out.

GORDO. Chaz –

CHAZ. What's going on?

GORDO. I found her outside. With – With –

INDIA. Bob. His name is Bob.

CHAZ. *That's* Bob?

INDIA. He's a Polish dwarf.

CHAZ. That thing's from Poland?

INDIA. It's the name of the breed.

GORDO. She was trying to kill him.

CHAZ. WHAT?

INDIA. I wasn't –

GORDO. She put a plastic bag over his head.

CHAZ. You're lying.

INDIA. I took it off. I put it on but then I took it off. I wimped out – see? That's the point.

(**INDIA** *deposits Bob in the bathroom.*)

GORDO. *(running in circles around the room)* She was outside by the garbage cans. All sneaking around. I'm telling you, Chaz, if I wasn't there she was going to suffocate that thing. She's a criminal. She's probably wanted by the F.B.I. at this point. She's probably plotting to kill us from the bathroom right now prying the faucet off to use as a weapon.

INDIA. *(returning from the bathroom)* I told you. I didn't go through with it.

CHAZ. Why were you trying to kill it in the first place?

INDIA. You don't understand. It's just so ridiculous – See, my Dad actually *walks* him. On a leash. He actually puts a rabbit on a leash, like he's one of those little toy dogs, and the two of them go bouncing up and down Lexington Avenue. Every day. Every morning. It's the most offensive thing you've ever seen. With those little beady eyes. And that sad little nose. It's just. AGGGHHH. It makes me so angry. Because I didn't ask for it. I didn't ask to be associated with all this. This – this – stuff. It was just given to me. Like a tattoo. Like a giant birth mark on my face that everyone can see. UGH – I HATE THE WORLD. I hate it!

(a moment)

CHAZ. Can't you just – let him go.

INDIA. I can't. He's a house pet. He wouldn't survive.

CHAZ. Oh.

INDIA. He'd get eaten by a hawk.

CHAZ. Hawks. Forgot about those.

INDIA. He's pathetic. He's just this helpless little thing my father bought from a breeder in Vermont.

CHAZ. Maybe you should just give him back.

INDIA. I can't. I know it sounds stupid but, it's just something I've got to do. For my own sanity and independence.

GORDO. Your sanity is a little suspect right now. It's in a different solar system.

INDIA. *(under her breath)* At least I wasn't dumping letters in the trash.

GORDO. NO!

CHAZ. What?

INDIA. He was pouring that box into a garbage can. I totally saw it.

GORDO. No.

> *(**CHAZ** stares at him.)*

CHAZ. What were you doing Gordo?

GORDO. I –

CHAZ. Tell me.

> *(a moment)*

GORDO. *(meek)* I was throwing them in the trash.

CHAZ. Why would you do that?

GORDO. I don't know.

CHAZ. Stop mumbling. Tell me why?

GORDO. She was trying to kill an innocent creature and you want me to explain why I was tossing out a few pointless letters?

CHAZ. They're not pointless to me. You know that.

GORDO. Yeah, but –

CHAZ. But what?

GORDO. Why do want to discover some mystery relative of ours who doesn't even know we exist? It's stupid.

CHAZ. To you.

GORDO. To everyone.

CHAZ. It doesn't matter why. It's just something I want to do.

GORDO. So you can tell them about me?

CHAZ. What?

GORDO. So you can ask them to come take care of me?

CHAZ. Why does it always come back to you?

GORDO. Why else then?

CHAZ. I DON'T KNOW – OKAY. I don't know.

GORDO. That's right. You don't know.

CHAZ. So. Wait. All of them? You've been doing this to ALL OF THEM?

(**GORDO** *doesn't respond.*)

HOLY…I'm gonna…all of them? For the past…

(**GORDO** *just nods.*)

FUCKIN – AGGHGH.

GORDO. I'm sorry.

CHAZ. YOU ARE SO…

GORDO. I'm sorry Chaz.

(**CHAZ** *goes over to* **GORDO***'s desk and flips it over. Toys go flying. Things break. It's a mess.*)

CHAZ. I need to go.

GORDO. Chaz –

CHAZ. I need to take a walk.

(**CHAZ** *exits.*)

INDIA. You are soooo dead.

GORDO. Shut up.

INDIA. You tried to sabotage your own brother.

GORDO. You're an animal killer. You have no soul.

INDIA. I thought it would be so easy. You know, to get rid of him. Stick a plastic bag over his head and not have to look at him ever again. But it's so different in reality – doing something like that – it's so different than just the idea of it.

(*beat*)

INDIA. Wanna hold him?

GORDO. Bob?

INDIA. Yeah.

GORDO. (*looking in the direction of* **CHAZ**) I – uh.

INDIA. I can't look at him anymore. He knows how I feel

about him.

GORDO. What if I drop him?

INDIA. He'll land on his feet. He's pretty good about that.

GORDO. Okay.

> (**INDIA** *hands* **GORDO** *the rabbit. It's awkward at first...*
> *He pets Bob uncomfortably.*)

INDIA. See?

GORDO. He's soft.

INDIA. I know.

> (**GORDO** *pets Bob.*)

INDIA. You wanna keep him?

GORDO. *Keep?*

INDIA. Yeah. I'm not bringing him with me.

GORDO. But what about your Dad? Won't he be upset?

INDIA. Probably. But don't worry – he's not going to have to check into a psycho ward or anything. He'll probably just buy another weird pet/symbol of perversity. Like a cobra. With a tiara.

GORDO. I don't know how to take care of something like this.

INDIA. Well. You'd need to feed him.

GORDO. Feed him what?

INDIA. Carrots. Raisins. Hay.

GORDO. Carrots. Raisins. Hay.

INDIA. And he doesn't like to be left alone all the time.

GORDO. Doesn't like to be left alone.

INDIA. Have you ever watched Animal Planet?

GORDO. I used to.

INDIA. See? You're perfect.

GORDO. Could I sleep with him sometimes?

INDIA. With Bob?

GORDO. Yeah.

INDIA. I don't think so. You'd probably smother him. You're a pretty big guy.

GORDO. Oh.

INDIA. And you've got to make sure to cover the floor. He poops all over the place.

GORDO. *(sympathetic)* Yeah?

INDIA. Uh huh.

GORDO. Poor Bob. Nobody likes him.

(**GORDO** *pets Bob.*)

(singing) Nobody likes you, everybody hates you why don't you go eat worms.

INDIA. So you're okay? You think you can handle him?

GORDO. What?

INDIA. I've got to finish packing. I just want to make sure you're ok.

GORDO. Okay...

(**INDIA** *exits.*)

(singing) Fat ones, skinny ones, smart ones, stupid ones, worms that squiggle and squirm.

Hi. My name is Gordo. Rhymes with *Board-o*. What's your name? Oh yeah. Bob. Maybe we can name you something else. If you're going to live with us. Guess what? I did something bad to my brother. Chaz. You'll meet him. He watches out for me – just like I'm gonna watch out for you from now on. He's great. He's very patient with me. Very patient.

(**GORDO** *pets Bob as the lights fade.*)

6.

*(Very early. In pre-dawn darkness. The living room is empty. Enter **INDIA** with all her bags. She goes over to **CHAZ**'s desk, picks up a piece of paper and a pen and starts writing a note. While she's writing, **CHAZ** enters. Fully dressed, with an overnight bag draped over his shoulder.)*

INDIA. I was just writing you a note.

CHAZ. Here I am.

INDIA. I was going to try to hitchhike or something. Since you didn't seem –

CHAZ. Last minute decision.

INDIA. Yeah – No – It's great.

*(**INDIA** crumples up the note.)*

CHAZ. I didn't take that much stuff. I packed in the dark.

INDIA. We can pick up stuff along the way, that could be fun.

CHAZ. Sure.

INDIA. Maybe like – cowboy hats. Some sort of festive disguise.

CHAZ. Do you have a road map? Any sort of itinerary planned out?

INDIA. No. Why – Do you think we need one?

CHAZ. I guess we could just keep driving west?

INDIA. See? You were totally harboring all this secret spontaneity, I knew it. Plus – it'll be harder for my dad to find us if we're just zig-zagging from one random place to the next.

CHAZ. Right.

INDIA. We should go. Before he wakes up.

CHAZ. Okay. I'm ready.

INDIA. Okay.

*(She puts her backpack on. **CHAZ** takes one last look around the room. They exit.)*

(The sound of the front door closing.)

*(In the darkness, we hear **GORDO** stirring.)*

GORDO. Chaz!?

*(Some rumbling. A few moments later, **GORDO** emerges from his room wearing a pair of corduroy pants and a tie. He struggles to tuck in his shirt as he dashes from room to room looking for Chaz.)*

GORDO. Chaz!

*(He checks **CHAZ**'s room.)*

Chaz?

(He checks the kitchen.)

Chaz?

(He checks out the front door.)

(A moment of realization, then panic.)

*(**GORDO** goes to his Time Out Chair. He sits, trying to find the sense of calm and comfort it once provided him.)*

*(**GORDO** jumps up from the chair. He looks around the empty room. His legs collapse under him. He sits in one big tangled mess for a moment and then very slowly, very delicately lowers the rest of his body to the floor. He lies like this for a long time.)*

(Time passes.)

(Lights shift to dawn.)

(More time passes.)

(Then – the sound of the front door.)

*(**GORDO** sits up.)*

Chaz!

*(After a moment, enter **CHAZ**, still carrying the overnight bag. **CHAZ** looks at **GORDO** in a loss for words. **GORDO** looks at the bag.)*

Chaz?

(**CHAZ** *looks at the overturned table. He flips it back over and begins picking up stray parts from the ground.*)

GORDO. Sorry about the letter thing. I'll be a lot better from now on. You'll see. A brand new Gordo. I'm gonna make an effort now. The Little Engine That Could. Things are going to be different around here. I promise you. No more bad things okay? They're in the past. They're *so* over with. No more just running around like a crazy man.

CHAZ. Yeah?

GORDO. Yeah. For real.

(*beat*)

CHAZ. Here. Come help me with this.

GORDO. Okay.

(**GORDO** *starts to move – then notices something. He goes over to his time-out chair, brings it over to the restored table and replaces his makeshift stool.*)

(*Together they pick up the stray pieces on the floor – Bingo chips, etc.*)

(**GORDO** *returns to his own desk. He unplugs the typewriter, sets it on the ground.*)

GORDO. Hey Chaz.

CHAZ. Yeah?

GORDO. You're a good brother. You take good care of me.

(*pause*)

CHAZ. We might have to get you a new desk. Something more stable. With actual legs.

GORDO. Yeah. Okay.

(**GORDO** *and* **CHAZ** *continue to straighten up their respective desk areas as the lights fade.*)

End of Play.

Printed in the United States
210132BV00006B/1-6/P

9 780573 663086